POWER FOR TODAY

Shirley A. McGarrell, Ph.D.

TEACH Services, Inc.
PUBLISHING
www.TEACHServices.com • (800) 367-1844

World rights reserved. This book or any portion thereof may not be copied or reproduced in any form or manner whatever, except as provided by law, without the written permission of the publisher, except by a reviewer who may quote brief passages in a review.

The author assumes full responsibility for the accuracy of all facts and quotations as cited in this book. The opinions expressed in this book are the author's personal views and interpretations, and do not necessarily reflect those of the publisher.

This book is provided with the understanding that the publisher is not engaged in giving spiritual, legal, medical, or other professional advice. If authoritative advice is needed, the reader should seek the counsel of a competent professional.

Copyright © 2019 Shirley A. McGarrell
Copyright © 2019 TEACH Services, Inc.
ISBN-13: 978-1-4796-0857-7 (Paperback)
ISBN-13: 978-1-4796-0858-4 (ePub)
Library of Congress Control Number: 2019938577

Texts marked (AMP) are taken from the Amplified Bible. Copyright © 2015 by The Lockman Foundation, La Habra, CA 90631. All rights reserved.

Texts marked (KJV) are taken from the King James Version. Public domain.

Text marked (NIV) are taken from the New International Version®, NIV® Copyright ©1973, 1978, 1984, 2011 by Biblica, Inc.® Used by permission. All rights reserved worldwide.

Texts marked (NKJV) are taken from the New King James Version®. Copyright © 1982 by Thomas Nelson. Used by permission. All rights reserved.

Texts marked (RSV) are taken from the Revised Standard Version of the Bible, copyright © 1946, 1952, and 1971 the Division of Christian Education of the National Council of the Churches of Christ in the United States of America. Used by permission. All rights reserved.

Published by

TEACH Services, Inc.
P U B L I S H I N G
www.TEACHServices.com • (800) 367-1844

DEDICATION

This book is lovingly, dedicated to our three children: Fenton Andre, Fern Althea, and Faith-Ann Abiola, and our four grandchildren: Safiya, Stephen, Marcello, and Gabrielle, with the hope that they will always be conscious of the Power of God that dwells within them

Power for Today is also dedicated to all humble readers who feel unworthy of being used by a Great God, powerfully.

TABLE OF CONTENTS

A Word from the Author vii

Acknowledgements ix

Power to Forgive 10

Power Sufficient for Weakness 14

Power to Be Humble 18

Power to Display God's Glory 21

Power to Be Ordinary Yet Different 23

Power to Be Poor in Spirit 26

Power to Believe 29

Power to Trust God's Guidance 33

Power to Do the Seemingly Impossible 36

Power to Be Fearless 39

Power to Experience the Superlative 42

God's Power as the Foundation of Wisdom 46

Power to Trust God with Your Life 49

Power to Be an Overcomer 51

Power to Shine 54

The Power of God's Kingdom 58

Power to Be Holy 60

Power to Be Strong 63

Power to Fight Back 66

Power to Be Kind 69

Power to Say "No" to Depression and Despair 75

Power to Give and Accept Love 79

Power to Live When Others Do Not Understand . . . 83

True Power 86

Power of Hope 89

God, the Greatest Empowerer 93

Power to Endure 96

The Power to Overcome Obstacles 104

The Power of Prayer 107

A WORD FROM THE AUTHOR

"**Power**"—what a powerfully effective word! It is a word that is vast in its meaning, and implies a possession of control, authority, and influence over others and situations; an ability to act or to produce an effect; strength to survive difficulties; physical might; mental or moral efficacy; and a source or means of supplying energy, among other things. When one has power, he or she has great strength and influence. This is what political and other societal, public, civic, and chief administrators crave, and will do anything to achieve and demonstrate it.

The type of power addressed in this small volume, however, is not that of the above; rather, it is one that is the opposite; it is one of a deeply spiritual nature—the power to do things that are not easy to do under normal circumstances. This might include, for example, the inner power and strength to be patient with those who are naughty in their conduct; forgiving those who do not deserve to be forgiven; strength to endure great trial, and to keep on trusting God to perform the seemingly impossible—those times when no positive sun appears in one's sky; to be able to smile even when the heart feels ready to cry; to see

God even in the darkness of night. This is unusual power! Conversely, it does not draw attention to its possessor, but instead, to the greatness, goodness, and majesty of a mighty God, who alone possesses it, and can give it to anyone who trusts Him, upon request. His promises are all true, and He is committed to the Word He has given to all His followers: *"Most assuredly, I say to you, whatever you ask the Father in My name He will give you"* (John 16:23, NKJV).

One does not, therefore, have to be in a position of public fame, or to be the inheritor of a noble, honorary birth. Not at all! Only the simplest and humblest Christians can be the possessors of this divine, spiritual power, for it is a gift from God alone; and when demonstrated, it has a unique and mystifying influence on the lives of the beholders—to the saving of their souls.

ACKNOWLEDGEMENTS

It is with joy that I acknowledge the contributions of my husband of over fifty-six years, Dr. Roy Israel McGarrell, to this small book on "Power." His insights shared with me from being a church pastor of many congregations, both small and large, for approximately twenty-six years have helped me greatly, along with twenty-five-plus years as a University Instructor/Professor, Administrator, and Dean of the School of Theology and Religion at Caribbean Union College, now the University of the Southern Caribbean (USC), located in Trinidad.

Also, I would like to acknowledge the editorial services of Ms. Bernice James, a friend of many years, and teaching colleague in the Department of English at USC. Ms. James' specialty lies in the areas of Rhetoric and Composition. Her consummate skill of keenness, and "eye for detail" have always been an inspiration to me through the years. Additionally, she is a growing and striving Christian woman who enjoys a living and active relationship with her Creator, Sustainer, and Redeemer—God.

Finally, I want to thank our Divine Father, the Great Giver of all knowledge, and Source of all Inspiration. His unlimited love and power have, in a large measure, enabled me to accomplish this project.

POWER TO FORGIVE

*"And forgive us our debts as
we forgive our debtors."*
(Matt. 6:12, NKJV)

God has empowered us to do many things—including taking the good news of salvation to lost souls. This can be done in a variety of ways. It is not only through large evangelistic crusades and the electronic, technological, and the social media, but also by one-to-one living testimonies and a quiet Christian life. One of the greatest areas of empowerment that He has granted us, however, is the power to forgive those who hurt us. This is not a simple gift—it is a priceless one! Those who receive it from God demonstrate a power that is enviable.

It is a simpler matter to forgive those who seek our forgiveness, for even though we hurt, at least they have asked. The challenge comes when we must forgive those who wrong us and they do not seek our forgiveness. How many times should we forgive a friend, a supervisor, administrator, son, daughter, parent, husband, or wife? Forgiveness, like charity, does look for limits, yet Heaven asks us to do as the biblical injunction advises, *"Do good unto all men"* (Gal. 6:10, NIV). The old maxim still stands true: "'There are times when it is better to be kind than to be right." Often, in the real sense of forgiveness, one cannot dwell on who was wrong and who was right, for then forgiveness would never occur—but when kindness supersedes rightness, healing on a higher level takes place. To be able to love, and to demonstrate kindness to those

> *It is a simpler matter to forgive those who seek our forgiveness, for even though we hurt, at least they have asked. The challenge comes when we must forgive those who wrong us and they do not seek our forgiveness.*

who have wronged us, is a power that can be acquired only from God, for the natural mind does not provide for this.

I had just given birth to our first child and had left the hospital for my parents' home in a small village in the country of Guyana, South America. Because of racial and political upheaval in the country at that time, it was difficult for my husband, who was working approximately seventy-five miles away, to visit me. The day he decided to make his visit to see his son, he was riding a bicycle from the city to the village where I was. This was because petroleum was scarce due to a country-wide political strike. When he was approximately six miles from home, three attackers of the opposite race saw him and proceeded to strike him with large pieces of logs. He fell off his bicycle and miraculously landed on his feet which enabled him to run for his life. Although he sustained injuries to his arm, this was nothing to be compared to what could have happened to him had he not landed on his feet—God allowed him to run immediately. He felt the assistance of angels pushing him forward and helping him outrun his attackers who wanted to kill him. Eventually, he arrived home safely, and was able to unite with the family and enjoy the arrival of his first child and son.

His ministry had members of both races, but never once did he mention this experience in any congregation since he never wanted to instigate animosity among the members of his congregations. God helped him to forgive the men of that race, instantly, although they could have taken his life. From then to today, God has allowed my husband to have close friends from that race as well as many others. We thank God for that power He has given to us all to forgive.

Today, if you want to experience the sweetest freedom, do not dwell on the hideousness of the act of another, and the difficulty of offering forgiveness. Just rest your case in the jacket of your Lawyer/Advocate—Jesus—and ask Him to give you that divine power to forgive. And He will!

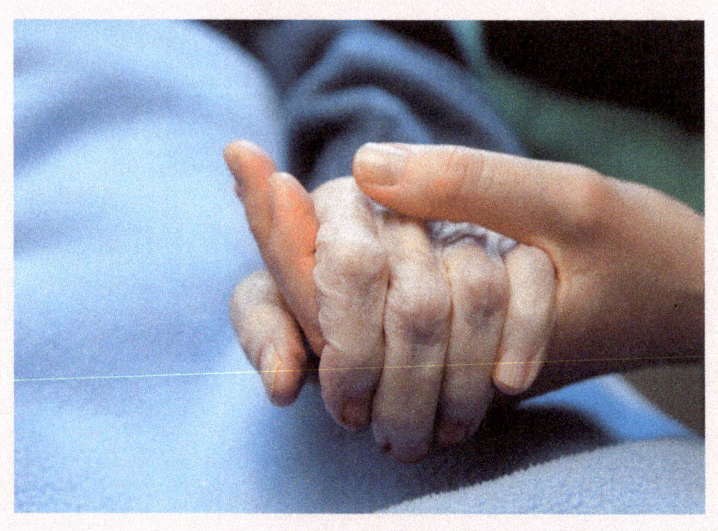

POWER SUFFICIENT FOR WEAKNESS

"My grace is sufficient for you, for my power is made perfect in weakness."
(2 Cor. 12:9, NIV)

The apostle Paul was here asking God, as most of us usually do, for something that was seemingly good—release from some sort of bodily affliction which was militating against his full ministry. God heard his prayer, but instead, gave him an abundance of grace to meet his needs. We never know why sometimes God works miracles, and, at other times, gives grace to cope with our crippling situations. The *Seventh-day Adventist Bible Commentary* discusses this: "Inward strength to endure is of a far mightier manifestation of the divine grace than master of the outwardly difficulties of life. Outwardly, a man may be torn, worn, wearied, and almost broken, yet inwardly, it is his privilege—in Christ—to enjoy perfect peace" (Vol. 6, p. 921).[1] It is an act of ultimate power to be able to accept one's condition—whatever that condition is—without resentment when the will of God is known, just as Christ was able to accept His Father's will with total resignation, in the Garden of Gethsemane.

Patrick Thomas was more like a Christ-figure in literary studies—a man of boundless energy, one who could have driven for sixteen hours cross-country without stopping at a rest stop, or even for a bathroom break. The harsh winters of Michigan never terrified him, for he hardly ever caught a cold. Everyone loved him for his magnanimous and altruistic spirit. But then one day, it happened! Without even feeling ill, he was informed by his physician that both of his kidneys had ceased to function. Patrick had to be on tri-weekly dialysis for four years with all the accompanying discomforts of changing the locations of shunts in order to facilitate blood withdrawals and transfusions.

---

[1] Review and Herald Publishing Association, Hagerstown, MD: 1980.

Furthermore, several bodily malfunctions occurred within that period that necessitated major surgical procedures which could have had seriously affected his joy in the Lord, but he allowed nothing to steal the joy that he found in Jesus. Neither did he allow this debilitating situation to limit his personal ministry of saving and influencing souls for God's kingdom.

Hundreds of prayers went up to Heaven on his behalf, and God gave him grace to meet all his needs: "… For added affliction, He [God] added His mercies, for multiplied trials His multiplied peace."[2] If one were to speak with him in person, or on the telephone, or via text and e-mail during those trying days, that person would have never known of Patrick's physical challenges, for praise to God dominated his entire being. God's power shines most and best in situations of weakness, and His strength is not diminished in the lives of those who trust in Him. His power has no boundary known unto man.

Several months after, Patrick quietly passed on to his final rest—a rest from which he will most certainly awake, in the not-too-distant future, when Jesus bursts into the sky with His glorious appearance. His life remains a wonderful testimony of love and trust in an all-wise God when things don't work as we would like them to.

---

[2] Hymn by Annie J. Flint, "He Giveth More Grace." http://1ref.us/rl (accessed 2/21/2019).

Today, if God chooses not to answer your prayer in a manner that you desire, do not worry; do not despair. Instead, trust His love, and watch how He will work for you to accomplish His will in a special way. The well-known preacher, Charles H. Spurgeon, reminds us in his sermon, "A Happy Christian," that, "The worldling blesses God while he gives him plenty, but the Christian blesses him when he smites him: he believes him to be too wise to err, and too good to be unkind; he trusts him where he cannot trace him; looks up to him in the darkest hour, and believes that all is well."[3]

---

[3]"The Happy Christian." *Metropolitan Tabernacle Pulpit Volume 13*. Sermon No. 736. http://1ref.us/rk (accessed 2/21/2019).

POWER TO BE HUMBLE

"I live in a high and holy place, but also with the one who is contrite and lowly in spirit, to revive the spirit of the lowly and to revive the heart of the contrite."
(Isa. 57:15, NIV)

It takes a lot of power to be humble—a power that only God can give, for He epitomizes it in illustrious ways. How can God—the Creator of everything visible and invisible—the One who inhabits eternity and dwells in an atmosphere that is perpetually holy—dwell also in the puny heart of a poor, sinful, wretched human being? God is so personal to all who call upon His name, opening their hearts and lives to Him. God is so instantly willing to save all who approach the mercy seat. He left the holiness and loftiness of Heaven and came to a cold, cruel, and calculating earth, riddled with sin and evil, and lived, died, and rose again so that sinners could be saved. This is true power!

Several years ago, when I served as the interim president of a small college in Trinidad, I was invited by an itinerant missionary professor, Dr. Chappala, to travel through a curvy, winding, and ditched terrain to a small one-bedroom shack where a family of eight lived. When I arrived and realized the abject poverty that surrounded this beautiful family—a struggling mother and seven children—I immediately felt an air of superiority—my position as against their condition. "Lord," I prayed, "please take away this feeling of self-pride, and give me the power to love this family vicariously." In an instant, God answered my cry to Him. Weak and puny people exult in self-pride; only powerful people can truly love. This power is given to us by God alone. It was not long after that members of our college faculty and staff were able to construct a beautiful two-bedroom, concrete house for this family, a place that they could happily call home. We turned the keys of this house over to them as tears of gratitude and joy flooded their eyes.

Christ is so unlike humans! He left the grandeur of Heaven and came to earth to be born of a woman—sinful and ordinary—so He could save all who come unto Him by faith, regardless of their social class, creed, circumstance, color, or character. Puny mortals get excited by their level of education, their monetary savings, and their professional positions on earth, which, in a moment, could fade into nothingness. As holy and as perfect as He is, Jesus Christ desires to dwell in your sinful heart. Therefore, open your heart's door and let Him in, and watch how He will work a miracle within you!

Thank God for His great power that allows Him to dwell by faith in your sinful heart today—a King supreme in your humble life.

Thank God for His great power that allows Him to dwell by faith in your sinful heart today—a King supreme in your humble life. Celebrate His beautiful presence! Experience His liberating power to revive you, and to give you power to love—yes, power to live!

POWER TO DISPLAY GOD'S GLORY

"They will be called oaks of righteousness,
a planting of the Lord for the display
of his splendor."
(Isa. 61:3, NIV)

God was calling Israel back to Him to be His special people, to showcase His glory. They were not to be just another set of people occupying space on earth; they were to be a powerful people—strong, sterling, beautiful, and righteous to display His glory. Oak wood is generally known as being a hard, stiff, and strong wood, and is, as a result, resistant in nature, as compared with other woods of the forest.

In Old Testament times, trees were often used figuratively to represent people. So, by extension, Israel was to be like the mighty oak—a special, righteous nation of people whose character reflected only the righteousness of their Creator, God. When the other nations of the world beheld them, they were to be an example of strength, resilience, and faith with a dazzling splendor that reflected only the beauty of the Lord.

God's desire for modern, spiritual Israel is no less today than it was in days of old. He longs to display in you the beauty of His character and the power of His love. It's nothing that you can do all by yourself; it is all that He can and will do through you if you open your life to Him. He can make you strong today to face any challenge, and He can make you a mirror to reflect His lovely character so that the office, the home, your classroom, or your workplace can become a better place today because of you. You have the power to be an agent for that change—today—for God has already given it to you.

Go forth, therefore, into this day with all its schedules, deadlines, and challenges, and feel the power that is yours to handle them all successfully!

POWER TO BE ORDINARY YET DIFFERENT

*"Where then did this Man get all this
[wisdom and power]."*
(Matt 13:56, AMP)

Jesus had just finished traveling through the towns in Galilee (Matt. 11) where He was teaching the people who followed Him through parables—the beautiful parables of weeds, the mustard seed, the hidden treasure, and the net—when He moved to His home town and began to teach the people in their synagogue. The people who assembled there to listen to Him with keen interest, saw something far different from the ordinary boy they knew as a child, and felt a sense of awe. They knew Him, for He had grown up among them. They knew His mother, earthly guardian, brothers, and sisters—a decent, but ordinary family. His words, manner, and demeanor, however, were powerful and impacting.

The more they listened, the more they were impressed, and were forced to ask each other: *"Where did this man get this wisdom and these miraculous powers? Isn't this the carpenter's son? Isn't his mother's name Mary, and aren't his brothers James, Joseph, Simon, and Judas? Aren't his sisters with us? Where, then, did this man get all these things?"* (Matt. 13: 55–56, NIV).

God's Holy Spirit allows "ordinary people" to be powerful. This power, however, is not one that is political or jurisdictional, not one of authority or superiority, but a power that is divine. The Holy Spirit's power is not dependent on one's education, neither on one's financial or social status. It has nothing to do with one's heritage or pedigree; rather, it has only to do with an established relationship with God, and a complete surrender to His will and the work of the Holy Spirit in one's life. The way to acquire it is simple: ask God to open your mind to receive it. He has already made it available to all.

He was just a young man when he came to our home for dinner one sunny, Saturday afternoon. After the meal, he said to my father, who was a church worker and a retired police officer, "Where do you get your power? I hear people in the village say that you are a powerful man, and they wonder at you."

"But you have seen that I am just an ordinary man, living a quiet life with my four children," my father responded.

"Yes," the young man insisted, "they see that, too, but they sense a strange power within and around you. Do you deal with any charm or strange force?"

"Yes," my dad insisted. "May I show you? Follow me."

The young man then tiptoed behind my father from the dining room, fearing that he would see some strange thing. He followed quietly until they both reached the master bedroom, and then my father showed him his family-sized bed, and quietly but firmly said to him: "Every time I kneel before this bed, I lay my life before the Lord, and ask for the Holy Spirit's presence and power. He has already heard and answered." Embarrassed and disappointed but trying not to show it, the young man said goodbye to our dad, departed, and thought on what he had just heard.

> "Every time I kneel before this bed, I lay my life before the Lord, and ask for the Holy Spirit's presence and power. He has already heard and answered."

Today, open your life to a Force outside of you, and a beauty of life and character will shine in a way that is compelling, arresting, and inspiring. Claim this promised power today, and watch God work in and through you!

POWER TO BE POOR IN SPIRIT

"Blessed are the poor in spirit for theirs is the kingdom of heaven."
(Matt. 5:3, NIV)

It is hardly likely, though not impossible, for the very financially rich person to be poor in spirit. This promise, therefore, is for the ordinary person who is content with his or her lowly state in life, and lives to please God and serve others. Jesus, in His teaching from the mount, proudly announces that those people are blessed or happy because they have a stupendous in heritance—an inheritance that surpasses anything that earthly monarchs, presidents, and world leaders can ever hope to have, and that is the inheritance of a Kingdom whose beauty and splendor exceeds one's greatest imagination. And God's promises are sure!

Rich people think and live in a certain way, and it is difficult for them to appreciate the poor. They may pity the poor, and deal their bread and money as a token of benevolence, but to be "poor in spirit" is to be more than financially deprived. "Poor," in this original sense, means those who are spiritually deprived and sense the need of a Savior, unlike the bigoted, self-righteous people who feel justified by their own works. Such people feel the need for God's grace, which is the "kingdom" to which Christ refers. When the "poor in spirit" receive this kingdom, there is joy immeasurable in whatever state they find themselves.

Gloria, a bright, beautiful, and blessed young woman, lost her husband through divorce in the prime of her youth. Outside of her newly-found relationship with God, she would have been devastated, but she knew God, and that made all the difference. A middle-management government worker in the corporate society, she carried herself with dignity, and made the Lord her personal companion. She could not wait for each day's duty to end so she could return home and talk with the Lord. Her personal testimony sometimes was: "I cannot wait to feel the warmth and love of my Savior." For her, "the kingdom of heaven," which is the kingdom of grace, was already hers. Sensing the need of a Savior, regardless of one's estate, is being "poor in spirit," and it is always the first step toward this glorious inheritance.

Such is a joy that no one, no circumstance, or no situation in life can steal, for such a joy is born of God. It, therefore, becomes a unique source of power that is available to you today—a power which, though financially rich or poor, can allow you to depend on Christ even in your own unworthiness. Then you can experience the delight, the joy, the happiness, and the blessedness that He showers upon us. Use this available power today!

POWER TO BELIEVE

"When he had gone indoors, the blind men came to him, and he asked them, 'do you believe that I am able to do this?' 'Yes Lord,' they replied."
(Matt. 9:28, NIV)

Of all the diseases most feared by man, blindness is among the worst. While it is true that many blind people have learned to cope with a world of darkness, and have accomplished great feats in this state, it is, nevertheless, still an indescribable and uncomfortable world in which to live. To be unable to see the loved ones who care for us in sickness, and to not be able to recognize the presence of friends would be discouraging to even the bravest soul. These are simple pleasures that help to make an otherwise sick person happy.

In our Scriptural reference today, Jesus had just raised the young daughter of Jairus from the jaws of death, and had healed the woman who had the issue of blood for twelve long years. Here He is in the home of one of His disciples, and two blind men have come to Him for healing so they may be able to see. They wanted to be able to see the tiny, multi-colored bugs that crawl on the leaves of low shrubs, and the glistering diamond-like dewdrops on the blades of grass in the early morning sunlight; to be able to see the mighty mountain range carpeted with rich, variegated green foliage and the winding highway that snaked through the hill city with grazing cattle on the left side, and fruit vendors on the right; and they wanted to be able to read the words of God's law, and not have to rely only on hearing the words spoken by others—these two blind men wanted to be able to see.

Most likely, they had heard of several acts of healing done by Christ and had the confidence in His power to do the *highly impossible* for them. So, they waited until they could find Him privately, and then they approached Him with their request. With eyes full of pity, mercy, and compassion, Jesus asked them: *"Do you believe that I am able to do this?"* To this they replied, *"Yes, Lord."* Jesus then touched their eyes and said, *"According to your faith will it be done to you"* (Matt. 9:29). Immediately their sight was restored. It was only as their faith was able to unite with God's divine power that they were able to receive a great miracle. Without the exercise of faith on their part, Christ would not have been able to exercise His power in their behalf.

This is one of the most exciting narratives in Scripture. Jesus then warned them not to tell anyone—but how could they not have done so when everyone around knew that they were blind? I have always believed that Jesus had an intrinsic sense of human behavior and very well knew that they would soon spread the news all around. Further, while He and His disciples were yet going away from the house where the healing had taken place, a man who was possessed by a demon and could not speak because he was stricken with dumbness, was taken to Him by friends who asked Jesus to heal him. Jesus touched him and healed him also, and immediately, he was not only rid of the demon that invaded him, but also he was able to speak clearly. The accompanying crowd went wild with excitement, for they had never seen or heard anything like that before in all of Israel.

All of these miracles, however, could have happened only because the afflicted ones believed that Jesus had the power to do them. Although centuries have rolled by since these amazing miracles, Jesus' power is still the same today, and He stands willing and ready to demonstrate this in your life—whatever may be your situation today. He wants you to be happy. He wants you to be free. However, you must first believe. Ask Him for the power that will enable Him to do so.

What rolls a dark cloud over the sun of your life today? Ask Him to dispel it, and believe that He can, and He will! Is it a broken relationship, a sick body, a wayward son or daughter, depleted financial resources, desire for a marital companion, or opportunity for educational advancement? Advance your request to the Father, and tell Him that you believe that He can. Imaginatively, in your private moments, listen to His voice when He says to your soul: *"Do you believe I am able to do this?"* Then, with a highly confident tone, let Him hear you say: "yes!" Then, listen again, and hear Him say: *"According to your faith will it be done unto you"* (Matt. 9:29, NIV).

Oh God of our many years, grant us this day the power to truly believe in You!

POWER TO TRUST GOD'S GUIDANCE

*"He [Jesus] guides me along the right
paths for his name's sake."*
(Ps. 23:3, NIV)

The power that God's children have today is the confidence that their Shepherd—God—will guide their footsteps each day in the paths of right doing and holy living. A good shepherd in the land of Palestine had to be familiar with the rough terrain when traversing the highlands of Judea, for often he would run suddenly into deep depressions on the path, and the sheep could be fatally hurt. Sometimes, he might have to lead the sheep in a path that may take longer to reach the pasture and pools of still waters. Knowing the way, therefore, is important for the good shepherd if he is to safely guide his sheep.

There is much anxiety when the way is not known. Many years ago, my husband, I, and another faculty colleague, made a trip to the southern part of the island of Trinidad. Returning home, however, we were forced to take a divergent route, which we thought we could comfortably negotiate and reach the highway in a shorter time. It was a route that we had never used before, and as we meandered through forested and isolated terrain, with only tall, huge trees and wild bush on both sides of the winding, twisting roads, we suddenly became anxious and afraid for own safety. Every turn we made, we hoped to see signs of the main highway, but we were disappointed at every bend. Finally, after what seemed like hours, we saw one house, and after several minutes, another, and this gave us hope that we were approaching civilization and home. Anxiety and fear immediately disappeared, and conversation, joy, and laughter returned among us. It was not long thereafter that we saw the lights of our home town. Reaching home brought us great joy, and we gave great thanksgiving to God.

Jesus, our Good Shepherd, knows the way that our lives should go, and He will guide us in the paths of righteousness. He promises He will do just that, for His own name and character are at stake. Wherever He leads today, therefore, is the right way even though it may seem long. He will never lead us along a path where there are dangerous holes, but we must permit Him to take the lead, and submit to His direction and care. Having this confidence in His guidance gives power to our lives, for we are confident that our faith and trust in Him will result in ultimate success.

POWER TO DO THE SEEMINGLY IMPOSSIBLE

*"With man this is impossible,
but with God all things are possible."*
(Matt. 19:26, NIV)

Peter was so happy to see Jesus! It was a joy that was indescribable, for he dearly loved Him. And so, amidst the storm, he shouted above the roar and din of the frightening waves, *"Lord, if it is you, bid me come"* (Matt. 14:28, RSV). And Jesus said, *"Come"* (vs. 29). Peter then leaped out of the boat and walked on the roaring waves toward Jesus. When he realized what he was really doing, he became afraid, and as the waves approached, he began to sink. Then he cried out: *"Lord, save me"* (vs. 30). Jesus grabbed him, and together they walked on the water and entered the boat to safety.

Could faith allow you to do the same? I often wonder, could I have had the courage to ask the Lord to bid me come in the midst of such a storm? Many times, I am so afraid to do the things which are normally, humanly possible; it is much more to ask the Lord to make me do the frighteningly impossible! Water has no foundation. But

Christ IS the foundation, and with Him, we are all similarly empowered.

My own desire for more education as a Faculty Dean in higher learning many years ago, along with the help and encouragement of my college president, caused me to enter into a doctoral program at the age of fifty-five. I confidently took all the available summer doctoral classes that were available at the university at which I was registered. I thought that I had it all under control—until I reached the point where I felt overwhelmed. There I was in my middle fifties, with little funding and highly challenging classes still to take. These included subjects like research, statistics, a doctoral comprehensive examination to prepare for and write a dissertation proposal. This not only included the writing, but also presenting and publicly defending.

> *Many times, I am so afraid to do the things which are normally, humanly possible; it is much more to ask the Lord to make me do the frighteningly impossible!*

I sat in the quiet of my home study and quietly wondered why I ever got started on such a program in my senior years. At worse, my college had already invested financially in my education, and I was afraid I would never complete it. I knew of several doctoral candidates who took many years to finish their programs, especially when they worked full-time. It was then that I, like Peter, said "Lord, save me!" Jesus' voice sounded above the storm waves of my confusion, and like He did with Peter, He took my hand, and we walked together on the stormy waves, and entered the ship of success.

In August of the year 2000, I graduated with a Ph.D. in Curriculum and Instruction (C&I), with an Advanced Cognate in English, from Andrews University, located in Berrien Springs, Michigan, USA. Since then, I have been privileged to serve in several top administrative positions effectively. God worked through me in reaching the minds of several young people and colleagues thereafter, in encouraging and helping them to do the seemingly impossible.

God gives to everyone the power to believe in themselves as long as they trust Him to accomplish difficult undertakings. We must allow Him to take our hands, for then what seems *impossible* becomes *possible*. Allow Him today to take your hand, and lead you every step of the way, remembering that *"with man, this is impossible, but with God all things are possible"* (Matt. 19:26, NIV).

POWER TO BE FEARLESS

"So, do not fear, for I am with you; do not be dismayed, for I am your God. I will strengthen you and help you; I will uphold you with my righteous right hand."
(Isa. 41:10, NIV)

The book of Isaiah reminds readers very poignantly of the power that is at their disposal. People who are fearless are powerful people! Do you remember when you were little, and the school bullies were always around to terrify you? Small, puny children were always afraid of them, for they were "big and bad." But the older and stronger children were never afraid of them. Those puny children loved to stay close to them for they were seen as being powerful and protective.

As a child growing up in a sheltered home, I was always afraid of such bullies, and my tiny physical frame made me a target for them. But my father was a policeman, and in those days policemen were very highly respected and feared in the community. Almost once every month, I had my poor father come to school in full uniform and speak with the headmaster about someone, usually a boy, who was a trouble to me. Now that I am so much older, and reflect on those days, I wonder why my dad used to listen so seriously to my complaints and made it a point to visit the school. However, when the bullies saw him, they knew they were in for much trouble, for those were the days when corporal punishment in an open and public manner was not prohibited in schools. I had power through my father, who was an officer of the law.

Today, God is reminding us that we have the greatest "fire power" accompanying us, so there is no need to fear; no need to be dismayed. Whatever our situation, He will strengthen us, and help us, and uphold us with His *"righteous right hand."* The "right hand" is symbolic of strength, endurance, and support; and this is not in the physical sense only, but more so in the sense of righteousness and true holiness. This is divine, omnipotent, omniscient, omnipresent, and omnificent or creative strength. So whether your challenge is of a physical, social, or mental nature, God is there to strengthen you. If you need instruction and guidance for a specific situation, He will be there to help you. If your strength is failing, and temptation and weakness are about to engulf you, He will be there to lift you up and uphold you. That is

> *Remember, it is always too soon to give up. Be a "warrior" and match your challenge with the power given to you by the promises of God!*

the type of power that is assured you if you, by faith, claim the promise.

Trust Him to do something for you today and feel that line of power surge through your soul. You are not a weak, frail, fledgling, but a strong and mighty mortal, for you are backed by an immortal and all-powerful God. Therefore, approach your challenge today with a confidence that is unmatched. William Wordsworth, in his poem *The Character of the Happy Warrior*, tells us that a warrior is one who challenges himself, one:

> Who, not content that former worth stand fast,
> Looks forward, persevering to the last,
> From well to better, daily self-surpast.[4]

Remember, it is always too soon to give up. Be a "warrior" and match your challenge with the power given to you by the promises of God!

---

[4]*The Character of the Happy Warrior*, by William Wordsworth, 1806, Public Domain.

POWER TO EXPERIENCE THE SUPERLATIVE

*"...Exceedingly abundantly above
all that we ask or think..."*
(Eph. 3:20, NKJV)

This verse has been a favorite of mine for many years because of the power that is implied. Here is power unmasked. It exposes God whose power knows no limit. He is so unlike the gods of the heathen—dead creatures or forms made of iron, brass, marble, or stone whose images shine, but cannot even blink much less think. The God of Heaven by whom all things consist is able to do for all His people that which is *"exceedingly abundantly above all that [they] ask or think."*

Abraham of old did not think that God was going to be able to make him the father of a son through whose seed the promised Messiah would come. He was very old and could not see the fulfillment ahead. And so, lacking trust, he declared: *"If only Ishmael might live under your blessing"* (Gen. 17:18, NIV). When Sarah became a mother in her old age, she said: *"God has brought me laughter, and everyone who hears about this will laugh with me … Who would have said to Abraham that Sarah would nurse children?"* (Gen. 21:6–7, NIV). Sometimes we pray for things over periods of years, until we tell ourselves, "It will never happen." Sarah waited for twenty-five years after God's initial talk with her husband, Abraham. But God fulfills His promises, even when it seems hopeless and impossible.

> God fulfills His promises, even when it seems hopeless and impossible.

It is sobering to pause and reflect on this mighty power of God, and to believe that His power is the same today as it was in the days of old. Often, our concept of God is limited by our intellectual and rationalistic view and understanding of life. But God has said: *"According to your faith, be it unto you*" (Matt. 9:29, KJV). He also says that if we would only have the faith of a grain of mustard seed, we would be able to say to that mountain, "*'move from here to there,' and it will move*" (Matt. 17:20, NIV). These are metaphoric expressions that heighten the impact of Christ's sayings—so that the force of His words could be felt, and readers' or listeners' experience could be vicarious. Metaphors are generally open-ended, so that anyone in any similar situation could place himself or herself there and experience the thrill of God. Place no limit on His power to perform the seemingly impossible in matters pertaining to life, remembering that all our petitions should be in accordance to His will and purpose for us.

Most and best of all, His exceeding abundant doings are His lavish gift of salvation for all who choose to cast their sins upon Him. By that one single act of surrender, eternal life and full and free salvation are made immediately available to all. This surpasses our greatest comprehension, but it is true. One can, therefore, live comfortably, and die peacefully, knowing assuredly that all is well with the soul. There is no greater joy, for the natural mind cannot begin to think of the glory that awaits us in God's eternal world of tomorrow. Isaiah declares: "*Since ancient times no one has heard, no ear has perceived, no eye has seen any God besides you, who acts on behalf of those who wait for him*" (Isa. 61:4, NIV). And John the Revelator concludes: "*Now I saw a new heaven and a new earth, for the first heaven and the first earth had passed away.... And God will wipe away every tear from their eyes; there shall be no more death, nor sorrow, nor crying. There shall be no more pain, for the former things have passed away"* (Rev. 21: 1, 4, NKJV).

Trust "the God of all superlatives" to perform the seemingly impossible for you today.

GOD'S POWER AS THE FOUNDATION OF WISDOM

"So that your faith might not rest on human wisdom, but on God's power."
(1 Cor. 2:5, NIV)

How often within recent times have you paused during the course of your life to reflect on the power of God? Every once in a while, it is therapeutic and emotionally and spiritually empowering to pause and think on God's omnipotent strength. Everything that the eyes could behold, and everything that is invisible, came into being because of God's power. He simply spoke, and everything came into existence by His word of command.

But the apostle Paul was saying more than this when he declared to his readers at Corinth that he did not want them to rest their faith on well-put-together words, intellectual discourses, or philosophical wisdom. Men and women have "*a way*" with words. They use them to persuade others into making decisions beyond their natural will. Paul had the power to do this—he held such a position of respect and authority in the early church—but he refused to do so. Instead, he wanted his readers to put their faith in the mighty power of God to change their lives, making them into a holy and sanctified nation of exceptional beauty. Only God's power can effect this change. A miracle of healing is indeed a wonder to behold, but a life that was headed toward destruction, and then veered toward salvation, through the power of prayer and the study of God's Word, is by far a greater wonder to behold. And God does this every day.

Faith today should not rest on what the pundits say, or the physicians' prognostications, but on the overriding control of God's power. Faith is not restricted by the wire fences of known or popular opinion. It has no boundaries, and it finds its resting place in the very throne room of God where power beyond human comprehension dwells. Illustratively, Peter walked on troubled water; Esther saved a mighty nation; David killed a great giant with a simple sling and small stone; Howard, a poor humble country boy, earned a Fulbright Fellowship that took him through graduate school; Ann Marie was completely

> *Faith is not restricted by the wire fences of known or popular opinion. It has no boundaries, and it finds its resting place in the very throne room of God where power beyond human comprehension dwells.*

healed from a diagnosis of uterine cancer without surgery or any form of therapy, and bore a healthy child as proof of healing; Michael, an outright confessed, sadistic murderer, repented and gave his life to Christ before he faced execution—all because of their incredible faith in God's power to save.

Whatever is your situation today, base your faith, not on what human wisdom concludes, but on what your faith in God's power can do. Remember that God's power knows no boundaries.

POWER TO TRUST GOD WITH YOUR LIFE

"… with man this is impossible;
but with God all things are possible."
(Matt. 19:26, NIV)

Today, you are placing your life in the hands of a God who is all powerful. His very hands *"laid the foundations of the earth, and His right hand stretched out the heavens"* (Isa. 48:13, NIV). This is what theologians call "anthropomorphism," where God is described in human terms to perform acts in human ways.

Look up to the heavens and see if you can guess where they begin and where they end. You can never do that! It's impossible! David describes the vastness of the heavens as God *"pitched a tent for the sun"* which is like *"a champion rejoicing to run his course"* (Ps. 19: 4, 5, NIV). Since God is the originator and creator of the heavens, the earth, the sea, and everything that dwells therein, we, His children, can experience great confidence and joy as we begin each new day of our earthly lives.

For most people, the right hand is the hand of strength. That is why God has promised to hold you with His right hand when you cannot carry yourself: *"For I the Lord your God, will hold thy right hand, saying unto thee, Fear not, I will help thee"* (Isa. 41:13, KJV).

Think about the power that lies in the hand of God as He touches you today, and as He deals with the circumstances and situations that you have entrusted to His care. May the awareness of this power allow springs of joy to break forth in your heart, as you, in turn, water the lives of others today. Depend on Him to take care of you. You will not be disappointed.

POWER TO BE AN OVERCOMER

"For everyone born of God overcomes the world. This is the victory that has overcome the world, even our faith."
(1 John 5:4, NIV)

Anyone who is an overcomer has power. We read of the young David, who, while attending his father's sheep, encountered a lion and a bear. These ferocious animals were going to destroy his sheep, but he, under the power of the great God of Heaven, was able to overcome them, and he ripped their jaws asunder. Later in his life, he was able to overcome and destroy a powerful giant who plagued the land of Israel and defied the power of the Living God. We also watch as the young, beautiful Queen Esther wielded a power over a weak and vacillating king, and changed the course of history, and saved the lives of an entire nation.

Everyone who is a Christian and has received the new birth experience and is "born of God," has been given power to overcome the troubles of this life. All of God's children are over-comers because they are born of Him; hence, they have power—power to do the impossible, to dare to stand for principle; they have power to subdue mountains, to calm situations and effect positive change where such is needed. This power comes through faith, and faith comes through the beautiful and mystifying act of prayer. No wonder William W. Watford, in his well-known hymn, "Sweet Hour of Prayer," declares:

> *Sweet hour of prayer, sweet hour of prayer*
> *That calls me from a world of care,*
> *And bids me at my Father's throne,*
> *Make all my wants and wishes known!*
> *In seasons of distress and grief,*
> *My soul has often found relief,*
> *And oft escaped the tempter's snare,*
> *By thy return, sweet hour of prayer.*

And the poet Phoebe Hinsdale Brown concurs by saying:

> *I love to steal awhile away,*
> *From every cumbering care,*
> *And spend the hours of setting day*
> *In humble grateful prayer.*[5]

Claim this power today to overcome your world of circumstance as you walk and talk with God right now in a living and dynamic relationship with Him.

---

[5] Phoebe Hinsdale Brown, "I Love To Steal Awhile Away," 1818.

POWER TO SHINE

"You are the light of the world. A town built on a hill cannot be hidden …. Let your light shine before others, that they may see your good deeds and glory your Father in heaven."
(Matt. 5:14, 16, NIV)

If you have light, you have power. God has made you the "light of the world," but the world is a big place, and you alone cannot brighten it. What you have the power to do, is to brighten the corner around you, by your life and light. And when all of God's people do this, the whole world will be illuminated. And so the command is given by the Creator of light to let your light shine so others will see your good deeds, and glorify not you, but your Father who dwells in Heaven.

As a young minister's wife, living in the main city of Guyana in South America—Georgetown—I had the privilege of making a spiritual call on the wife of a reputable attorney-at-law. Upon reaching her palatial residence in an upper-class neighborhood, I rang the doorbell to announce my arrival. The lady was not at home, but her attorney husband was. He was working at his desk in his study at the time; he got up, left his desk, and moved toward me, opening the door. Upon seeing me, he declared: "Madam, you are a powerful person; you have the light." *What light?* I wondered silently. Then he explained: "Just before you arrived, I felt my whole body shake. Then the doorbell rang. Madam, you have the light. You have the power." I later learnt that he was a Transcendentalist.

Since then, our children, who are now grown adults, still tease me when they cannot get me to agree with some of their decisions by saying: "Mom, we remember that you have the light; you have the power." Of course, this is just their own adult mischievous way of reminding me of that early experience.

Just as a candle lights the way in an area engulfed in darkness, so your light can make a difference to lives that are laden with care, doubt, disappointment, and fear. That gives you power—power to change a situation of darkness to a situation of light because of the hope that you bring by the love that you share. And when your own life becomes shrouded with darkness, God will lift the cloud with His power, thus causing the light of His presence to prevail. When people see this miracle, they will glorify the God of heaven.

> *Just as a candle lights the way in an area engulfed in darkness, so your light can make a difference to lives that are laden with care, doubt, disappointment, and fear.*

This is not a power that the Christian who possesses it could measure. It is not political, academic, or professional power. Conversely, it is humility—thinking of one's self not highly. It is a power to be discerning—to watch for, and to discern—opportunities to say that kind word, to do that kind act, to sympathize, to advise, and to counsel. It is smiling when your heart feels like crying, knowing assuredly that God can turn that same situation around miraculously. In this way, others will not see your tears; instead, they will see God's face shining like a light, even like the light of an angel.

Stephen of biblical times knew that he was facing death by the hands of cruel men who were stoning him for the cause of Christ. So, he turned his life over to the hands of his loving Creator and told those who were killing him what he was really seeing in his vision of heaven. In turn, God gave him that power as he faced death, and his face shone with a light from heaven. I am sure that those who were engaged in that unkind and cruel exercise could never have gotten that experience out of their minds even after his death.

Although his life was taken, the memory of his story remained a strong and continued rebuke to his destroyers, and as a result, one of them ultimately became an apostle of spiritual strength and power to the Christian world. That man was Saul, whose name was later changed to Paul. The Holy Bible would not have been, even today, what it is without the inspired writings and counsels of the great apostle Paul! It was at his feet that those who stoned Stephen laid their garments (Acts 7:58).

Let your light shine today by the joy that you share, and the hope that you radiate in spite of your circumstance, and experience intrinsic power!

THE POWER OF GOD'S KINGDOM

*"For the kingdom of God is not
a matter of talk but of power."*
(1 Cor. 4:20, NIV)

Many in the Corinthian Church, after Paul's departure from them, had become arrogant and boastful. He had taught them about God's kingdom by pious and gentle living, undergirded by a strong spirit of love for each other as well as for souls lost to sin. In his absence, certain among them laid claims to confident assertions of authority, and got carried away by positions of leadership, feeling that power to live and win souls lay in their ability to use words and wield influence.

Because of this situation, Paul sent Timothy—young and devout—to remind them of the true nature of power, for the kingdom of God is not a matter of talk, but of power—a power that is found only in love and a gentle spirit. The dynamite power behind the progress of God's church is the Holy Spirit of God, which is what draws men and women to Him.

Several years ago, after my husband, Roy, and I graduated with our undergraduate degrees from Caribbean

Union College, located in Trinidad, West Indies, Roy was assigned to serve as the pastor of a large congregation in the Upper Demerara River in Guyana, South America. As with Timothy in Corinth, many were looking at the young rookie, the intern minister, with little or no experience, as not a good replacement for the older, senior ministers for a large church congregation. The problem that faced the parish persisted for many years as seasoned, brilliant ministers came and went. But the new, young minister, Roy, embraced the challenge with pious and quiet wisdom, and within a period of six months, a roaring power soared through every row of adults and youth in that congregation. That church experienced a quality of love that was not known before. It is now over approximately forty years since my husband, Roy, and I left that congregation, but the members, many of whom are now very old, have never ceased to reminisce on the way the Holy Spirit broke up established factions, and destroyed the seeds of hate that were growing into poisonous plants within the confines of that city congregation.

The Kingdom of God, which is the Kingdom of Grace that is available to you and me today, is not built on educational, financial, or social status; it has nothing to do with authority or political prowess; rather, it is all about God's Holy Spirit's power, which is a still, small voice, and love that accompanies a quiet and gentle spirit. Feel that power surge through your soul as you face a new day!

POWER TO BE HOLY

"Be holy, because I am holy."
(1 Peter 1:16, NIV)

Although biblical critics tell us that that textual evidence is divided between the imperative (a command to be holy) and the future tense (a call to be holy), the intention of this verse is the same: God is calling His people to live a holy life. To be holy means to be set apart, or to be spiritually pure, to be given to prayer and charitable works, and to be godly. How can someone living in today's world be characterized as holy? All that God bids us to do, He enables us to do. The call to holiness is, therefore, not a frightening command, for holiness is a natural virtue that comes from a connection with the Source of holiness—Jesus Christ.

When I was a child, I saw this practiced in the life of my father, who, for all his working life, had been a military officer. Upon his retirement, he drew closer to God, and God pervaded the very fabric of his life. There was no isolation from people; instead, he fully integrated himself into the lives of all the people who lived around him—those in the street, in the village, and at church. Whenever he had to leave his home, he paused for silent prayer on his porch. Whenever he returned, he did the same thing. Before he drank water, or ate a meal, he prayed. As he showered in the bath, he prayed, asking that God's Holy Spirit would wash his life. Whenever he spoke with the neighbor across the fence, or had any other daily encounters, he looked for opportunities to share the love of God.

Often, holiness is associated with sinlessness, but no one is sinless. The holy person, however, does not cherish or enjoy sin, but shuns it like poison. He or she finds no joy in sinning because, according to the great apostle Paul, the *"life is hid with Christ in God"* (Col. 3:3, KJV). Sins that occur because of living in a state of sin are daily confessed, and Christ covers these with His blood. People will feel happy, comfortable, and inspired in their presence. Occasions for the expressions of anger, jealousy, and pride will always be there, but a conscience that is alive to their danger will always inform the heart and lead it to repentance.

There is joy in the life of one who lives in such close contact with God on a daily basis. A person living this life will not be odd or strange; rather, he or she will be one of the most inspiring people to be around, for his or her life is so much akin to the life of Jesus Christ. One is not primed up for holiness; he or she simply lives a life that is wholly dedicated to God and His service, and experiences and shares God's love in a manner that is invigorating, not passive; serene, not hostile; sensitive, not uncaring; pure, not defiling; hopeful, not discouraging; and happy, not obnoxious. The holy person daily senses the presence of God in his or her life, whatever the circumstances. As a result, there is always a spirit of joy, for *"in [His] presence is fulness of joy; at [His] right hand, there are pleasures forevermore"* (Psalm 16:11, KJV).

Today God has given you the power to be holy. Use it to His glory, so that your life can be filled with joy immeasurable.

Today God has given you the power to be holy. Use it to His glory, so that your life can be filled with joy immeasurable. That is why the hymn writer, W. D. Longstaff (1882), admonishes: *"Take time to be holy, speak oft with thy Lord; Abide in Him always, And feed on His Word."*

POWER TO BE STRONG

*"You then, my son, be strong in
the grace that is in Christ Jesus."*
(2 Tim. 2:1, NIV)

Paul, the great apostle and adopted father of Timothy, was reminding him of the natural source of power that was available to him as a young man. One does not have to be the recipient of lofty and accredited degrees, the holder of high credentials and positions, or the recipient of years of life's experiences in order to have access to this supreme power. The grace of God automatically gives this power—power to live above the ordinariness of sin, power to trust God's promises in situations where there is fear and anxiety. When others can see no way out, they can be encouraged and fascinated by the power of faith, and the confidence in prayer that they see reflected in such a person This power has its source in a relationship that one establishes in the great King of the Universe. He gives us power to believe, and power to trust, and these make a person stand out amidst a crowd of faithless and unbelieving others. This strength is supernatural. It is found only in the grace that is in Christ Jesus.

Grace is an abstract word, but concreteness is in its meaning. It is not nebulous. The word really means undeserved favor shown by God to everyone, through Jesus Christ. It begins with one's consciousness in recognizing God's immeasurable gift of salvation that produces joy in this life in spite of any circumstance, and the hope of eternal life when this life shall have passed away. The power inherent in this grace makes the life of anyone special. Just the presence of that person sanctifies a place and creates a whole new atmosphere when that one enters a room, a crowd, or a congregation. This power is not for self-exaltation, but for the glorification of God's name on earth.

Roy was just thirteen years of age, but when he was with his friends, there was always a restraint—they did not curse, swear, or plan bad activities simply because he was there. When they were by themselves in idle boys' talk, and he suddenly appeared on the scene of action, they knew they had to change the tenor of their conversation. Young Nevin had a similar power of influence. When family and friends were voicing grave concern over the critical situation of his beloved mother, who was dying from a rare disease in a Florida hospital, eight-year-old Nevin appeared, and the conversation ceased because they all knew that he had the faith that his mother would be healed because he had asked God to perform that miracle. The family could not, therefore, express doubt in his presence. Such is the power that is available even to the young. It was not long after that his mother was fully restored from her sickness.

That kind of power is available to you today, young and old alike, because it is vested in the grace of Christ Jesus. All you have to do is claim it. Experience the thrill of it today, and watch it work to bless others as well as increase your own joy as you experience this unique strength forever and always. Heed the imperative command from the Source of Grace and possess that power from God to be strong!

POWER TO FIGHT BACK

*"See, I will make you into a threshing
sledge, new and sharp, with many teeth.
You will thresh the mountains and crush
them, and reduce the hills to chaff."*
(Isa. 41:15, NIV)

When I was a little girl growing up in a small village in the country of Guyana, South America, it was customary for me to see manual laborers cutting away at grass for the feeding of cattle, or rice stalks to be gathered and sent to the rice mill for threshing. They used a grass knife. This was a very sharp, steel piece of equipment, shaped in the form of a half-moon with a wooden handle. With bent backs, these workers, with swipe after swipe of that knife, would cut all the grass or rice stalks, which were then gathered into bundles for their separate purposes.

Figuratively, Israel was the wheat to be threshed because of their disobedience to God's law. In this promise of power, however, Israel was eventually going to be the one who would become the thresher of the heathen nations around. This was a promise of power. God's people would do the impossible by not only threshing the mountains, but also by crushing them, and reducing them to oblivion. Nothing was going to be impossible for Israel to attain! The mountains and hills represented all the heathen and wicked nations around—enemies to be destroyed.

> *Whatever that formidable challenge may be, God is promising to give you the power to overcome it completely.*

Today, your mountain or hill may be the hidden—latent fear of failure; coping with health challenges; or dealing with loss through death. It may be a financial undertaking, an examination, a legal battle, or a decision that has life-threatening undertones. Whatever that formidable challenge may be, God is promising to give you the power to overcome it completely, like a sharp threshing sledge would do to wheat. And the victory would be so complete that you would want to know why there was that initial fear in the first place, for the mountain would become chaff under the powerful doings of God in your life. This promise of power to Israel of long ago is yours today for the asking.

Melanie did not know how she would survive staying in college as a young unsupported divorcee with two small daughters, but she claimed the power to crush that mountain. What was worse, however, was that when contending with the throes of financial registration at the beginning of fall quarter one particular school year, she received news from her homeland, that a near kin had lost his relationship with the Lord, and had succumbed to the pressures of life by taking the lives of all three of his children, his wife, and himself. That became a mountain that she could not easily crush, but with good support from faithful friends and caring church members, backed by God's promised power, she was able to remain in school, finished the semester, and was now on her way toward earning her coveted degree. At the time of writing, it is now several years since she graduated with a B.A. degree in the behavioral sciences. Her two little girls have since grown up into fine Christian young women, and are themselves working toward attaining their own bachelor's degrees in various academic fields.

Any hill or mountain can be crushed today because of God's promised power to you. Claim that power now!

POWER TO BE KIND

"Is not this the fast that I have chosen? to loose the bands of wickedness, to undo the heavy burdens, and to let the oppressed go free, and that ye break every yoke? Is it not to deal thy bread to the hungry, and that thou bring the poor that are cast out to thy house? when thou seest the naked, that thou cover him; and that thou hide not thyself from thine own flesh?"
(Isa. 58:6, 7, KJV)

What a lovely picture of what it means to be kind—giving to the poor; bringing relief to the unfortunate; untying the shackles of wickedness by bringing light to those who walk in darkness; granting freedom to those who are bound by the chains of sin; granting hope to the hopeless; giving clothing to those who have little or nothing to wear; providing refuge and housing to those who have nowhere to lay their heads, especially at night, and more. To the heart of Jesus, being kind is even greater than conforming to ritualistic fasting and ceremonial observances. He asks the rhetorical question: *"Is not this the fast that I have chosen?"* (Isa. 58:6). Showing kindness to others is precious to the Lord.

Being kind to others, however, does not come easily for many of us, and yet, for others who pride themselves on being kind to everyone, there are unconscious limitations in their minds that inhibit the transmitting of kindness. Being kind is one virtue that truly identifies those who love and serve the Lord, and it is also a vital exhortation from Him—our Kind, Loving, and Faithful Father in Heaven. He declares: *"And be ye kind one to another, tenderhearted, forgiving one another, even as God for Christ's sake hath forgiven you"* (Eph. 4:32, KJV). To be kind means to be loving and affectionate to others, to possess a sympathetic and forbearing nature, to be humane and empathetic, to be thoughtful, to be considerate, and to be willing to give to others at a cost to ourselves, among other things. These laudable practices are not always easy to perform, naturally, especially when we feel constrained to demonstrate these virtues to those who are not our friends, and to those persons who are hard to love because of their blatant foibles and conspicuous idiosyncrasies. It is easy to be kind to those with whom we normally associate, to people we know, as well as to those who are affable and gracious to us, but it is always a challenge to be kind to those who we do not know, those who are not within the orbit of our affection, and those who are not kind to us. In such cases, we need to ask God for the "power" to show and transmit kindness to those who fall within these and other negative categories.

There is great joy in being kind, for it blesses both the givers and the receivers. How can I ever forget one special day, many years ago, after I had struggled with books, note files, and journals in the library at Andrews University, located in Berrien Springs, Michigan, as well as in my apartment at Lamson Hall. I was preparing to write my doctoral comprehensives. Finally, the day arrived for the actual writing of the examination, which lasted several hours. On that significant day, my very close friend, Florence, sensing my mental and emotional anxiety, generously thought of doing me a kind and benevolent favour. She proceeded to cook a very special five-course, vegetarian meal for me, and then drove over to the residence hall to request of the Dean of Women, permission to leave her bounty in my room. The dean not only acquiesced, but accompanied her, to complete her act of kindness.

After entering the room, the resident dean and Florence cleared off the books, files, and papers that I had on the table, which was also my writing desk. They laid all of my paraphernalia neatly in a corner on the floor, and together they spread upon the table a colourful and appropriate tablecloth along with napkins and cutlery to accompany the food that Florence had prepared. The dean then re-locked my room, and Florence drove away.

After my examination was over, I had trudged home to my residence hall room from the classroom in the education building, where I had been for several hours. I just wanted to lay down my handbag, and then go to the snack bar to source some food before taking a nap. Finally, I reached my door, turned my key, and there, what a stupendous surprise! Instead of my rugged and confused-looking table on which I had left books, files, and papers of all types, I saw a banquet table! It was a "wow" and euphoric experience for me. I could not believe the reality! "Who had done this?" I wondered. How could that person have gotten into my room when I was sure I had locked my door? Why the "banquet-type" spread? Was it the act of an angel? In the midst of my wondering, my telephone rang, and I heard the well-known voice of my residence hall dean, who told me the whole story. The joy that I experienced was unspeakable. To be kind is to be thoughtful of others. Yes, Florence was a true and solicitous friend!

The challenge, however, comes when we sense our weakness to be kind not only to the lovely, but also to the unlovely, as Jesus was when He dwelt on earth, and continues so to be now in the courts of heaven. This is not always naturally attainable. Joe was a very brilliant and talented young, graduate student, who was always in need of assistance—financially and otherwise—and whenever his impecunious condition reached an embarrassing level, he would penitently approach me seeking aid, and I spared no pains to help him. I assisted him regularly, but he possessed a very critical and abrasive personality which negated the desire to help him spontaneously. On one particular occasion, he erroneously judged me for being party with the administration of the university concerning a decision which he considered hostile to him, and, to vent his anger, he proceeded to be abusive and called me a name that was very unbecoming, unjustified, and unkind. I was severely hurt. There and then I determined that I would no longer be kind to him.

The following morning, however, he returned to my office to request financial help, and also to seek pardon and forgiveness for his misdemeanour the day before. I accepted his request for pardon, and asked God to help me not to withhold my benevolence from him. God heard my prayer, and gave me strength to be truly kind to him. I gave him what he needed, and I felt blessed.

When we ask God for that power, we will be able to demonstrate love, care, and kindness to all, regardless of reciprocity. Although it may take great sacrifice of funds, personal pride, and emotions, we will be able to give a smile to those who may not return one to us; forgive those who have spoken evil of us; pardon those who have betrayed us; give funds and food to those in need; show kindness by giving care to dumb animals that cannot articulate as humans do; give shelter as much as we can to the homeless; and still share the gospel of Jesus with those who are unmindful, unwilling, or even unyielding to hear about Him and His love for them.

God will give us that power to be kind, both to the lovely and the unlovely, when in faith and with confidence we ask Him for the potential to witness for Him. Trust Him to do that!

POWER TO SAY "NO" TO DEPRESSION AND DESPAIR

"Then Paul answered, 'why are you weeping and breaking my heart? I am ready not only to be bound, but also to die in Jerusalem for the name of the Lord Jesus.' When he would not be dissuaded, we gave up and said, 'the Lord's will be done.'"
(Acts 21:14, NIV)

The great apostle Paul was making his final rounds through various countries, along with his disciples, en route to Jerusalem. Although he knew what fate awaited him there, he pressed on with God's power to face the earthly end of his divine calling. While passing through the then-known world, including Thessalonica, Berea, Athens, Corinth, Ephesus, Macedonia, and Greece, he was teaching, preaching, and healing the sick and those possessed by demons. Finally, he was now ready to leave for Jerusalem. At their last stop on the voyage to Tyre, they were greeted warmly by the brethren there. They stayed at the house of Phillip, the evangelist. After they had been there a number of days, a prophet by the name of Agabus came down from Judea and visited the house where they were.

Agabus then took Paul's belt and tied his own hands and feet with it and said, *"Thus saith the Holy Ghost, so shall the Jews at Jerusalem bind the man that owneth this girdle, and shall deliver him into the hands of the Gentiles"* (Acts 21:11, KJV). When Paul's disciples and others who were with him heard these words from the prophet, they became fearful and pleaded with Paul not to go up to Jerusalem. They pleaded until they cried. After Paul watched them and heard them, he said to them in tones sad and low: *"Why are you weeping and breaking my heart? I am ready not only to be bound, but also to die in Jerusalem for the name of the Lord Jesus"* (Acts 21:14, NIV). When they realized that he would not be dissuaded, they wiped their eyes and said, *"the Lord's will be done"* (Ibid.).

It was only human that the great apostle Paul, upon hearing their words and watching them weep for him, was discouraged. It caused him to despair of the ugly and frightening reality of an awful and cruel death, but God gave him the power to say "no" to depression and despair. The journey of life is filled with travelers who run into serious occasions that cause them to become weary, frightened, depressed, and full of despair, and hence to easily succumb to these challenges, which, when they do occur, can make life joyless. These occurrences could take place during any stage of life—childhood, young adulthood, middle life, and old age. No one is exempt from these journeying "potholes," unless God gives us the power to say "no." Under such circumstances, encouragement from others, along with the strengthening assistance of the Holy Spirit, allows us to jump over these ditches, as we, like the great apostle Paul, *will* our minds to say a resounding "no." It's an intrinsic power given to us by God, and God alone.

> *It was only human that the great apostle Paul, upon hearing their words and watching them weep for him, was discouraged. It caused him to despair of the ugly and frightening reality of an awful and cruel death, but God gave him the power to say "no" to depression and despair.*

Jesus Himself struggled with this challenge in the Garden of Gethsemane, as He was about to endure the crucible of the cross. He cried out to the Father: *"Father, if thou be willing, remove this cup from me: nevertheless, not my will, but thine, be done"* (Matt. 22:42, KJV). It was then that God sent angels who ministered to Him in His resolve to say "no" to discouragement, and "no" to despair. As power was given to Him, so power will also be given to us when we run into those destructive potholes on the road of life, when we are fighting both with our own emotions and with those who care, and we tend to give in and to give up.

May God grant us all that power to always say "no" to discouragement and "no" to despair.

POWER TO GIVE AND ACCEPT LOVE

*"A new command I give you:
Love one another. As I have loved you,
so you must love one another."*
(John 13:34, NIV)

The power to love is as strong as the power to forgive. Not everyone can love, for many were not taught how to do so, and have seldom, or never, experienced love enough to know how to impart it. Several years ago, when I served as a student secretary in an institution of higher learning, I was given a junior helper to assist me in running errands, as well as doing small chores that I was too busy to do. This beautiful young woman could not understand why, and how, I was so full of love. For me, whatever I was doing or saying was so ordinary—that was how I knew myself to be, but to her, this was extraordinary. Many years elapsed since our experience of working together, and our lives took different courses. I returned to my homeland in the Caribbean, and she went on to acquire proficiency in another language, then returned to the University to complete her degree program.

Coincidentally, after many more years, we surprisingly encountered each other at our Alma Mater. It was then that she told me her sad story of not being able to acquire that ability to love, even after separating from me. She attributed this lack to the fact that she had not received much of it during her childhood; therefore, she did not know how to give it to others. This disillusionment led her to the point of attempting to take her life. But, providentially, God allowed a kind, loving, and caring Christian couple with whom she stayed during the year she was acquiring a foreign language, to discover her lying on her bed in a state of unconsciousness, and they provided the needed medical intervention. This experience brought her to the full realization that she needed the help of a God whose main attribute is love—One whose name is equivalent to love, for God is love. Today, this lady's life radiates with love, and she has become a loving, kind, and caring Christian professional woman—one with whom others love to associate, and one whose heart now overflows with love for her fellow person.

Love is of God, and He is love. When we demonstrate love for each other, it is a sign that we are God's children and His disciples. God's Holy Word says, *"By this shall all men know that ye are my disciples if we have love one for another"* (John 13:35, KJV). It is a gift from God. Love is shown by words, actions, and deeds. When we can genuinely say to someone who is experiencing a difficult time, "Hold on: don't give up;" when we can offer intercessory prayer in his or her behalf; or when we do a kind act or deed—these are demonstrations of love. Many people have nights with no daybreaks on their horizon. During these times friends can remind them that God is with them in the darkness just as He is with them in the light. Do not try to understand; just trust Him, for nothing enters into one's life unless it passes through His filter. His love is always shining whether it is in darkness, or light.

On the other side of the *"power to give love"* spectrum, we must ask God to also grant us the power in our lives to *"receive and accept love."* This is not always easy to do. Sometimes, personal pride and haughtiness of spirit stand in the way of our being open to receive from others tokens and other expressions of love. Especially is this so when the personages of those who offer tokens and expressions of love lie in contra-distinction with how we see and evaluate ourselves in our own eyes. These *"givers"* may be perceived by us as being poor and ordinary people. Such judgments and evaluations may grow out of the murky, perceived soil of racial superiority, financial and social status, religious affiliation, and professional bearing. The power and ability to accept expressions of love from others, regardless of their status in life, is a gift from God. Happy and blessed are those who can freely give love, and those who are humble enough to receive expressions of love from others, regardless of heritage.

It was the poet Robert Browning who thoughtfully posited: "Take away love, and this world is a tomb," and it was the physician, William Menniger, who repeatedly declared: "Love is the medicine for most of mankind's ills." Most importantly, however, love is Jesus Christ Himself! May God grant us that power in our lives to both experience and demonstrate His love.

POWER TO LIVE WHEN OTHERS DO NOT UNDERSTAND

"But after he had considered this, an angel of the Lord appeared to him in a dream and said, 'Joseph, son of David, do not be afraid to take Mary home as your wife, because what is conceived in her is from the Holy Spirit.'"
(Matt 1:20, NIV)

Many times in our emotive emphasis on Mary and the sweet baby Jesus as we allow ourselves to be caught up with the mystique of the nativity, we tend to bypass the strength and role of Joseph. Joseph could not understand what was happening with his young fiancée, Mary, but since he loved her sincerely, he did not want to expose her to shame and ridicule. He had just reached the point of deciding how to put her away quietly. While he was yet brooding over the problem that perplexed him sorely, God gave him a dream. Inspired dreams are Heaven's media of communicating illuminating insights, and Joseph knew that he was not to question Mary's virtue and that her pregnancy was of divine origin.

He knew what he had to do, and he did it. Hence, in the genealogy of Jesus, he became a member of the royal line as recorded in the Gospel of Matthew.

The reality, however, was that Joseph had to continue to live in a society where such a situation was not accepted as a social norm, and was looked upon with askance by both the common people and the genteel society. No explanation on his part could have convinced them otherwise. One has to have inner strength and power to live and work with people who may not understand the reason for a position you may have to take. That power was available to Joseph, and he embraced it. He knew what he had to do, and he did it. Hence, in the genealogy of Jesus, he became a member of the royal line as recorded in the Gospel of Matthew.

What a significant honor was awarded to him! To be able to live in a society when that means a family, church, neighborhood, office, or circle that doesn't understand what you know God has communicated to you, is an amazing thing. It takes strength and experience—a certain type of power—which God alone could give. Ultimately, truth will rise to the surface, and people will come to know and understand, just as everyone knows today, that the whole world is changed as a result of the birth of the Christ Child, Jesus. Such is not won, however, by trying to justify your actions, for even then, all will not understand the position you have taken.

If today you have to stand alone because of what you know is God's will for your life, remember that divine power is available at your call. God's power stands ready to strengthen your mind and steel your determination to live with comfort among those who may not immediately understand what is going on in your life. In His time, He will make all things plain; and your heart shall rejoice, and others will give praise to God with you.

TRUE POWER

*"The Lord Jehovah is
my strength and my song."*
(Isa 12:2, KJV)

When one has strength in a particular area, he or she automatically has power—power to effect; power to change. The power that a child of God has, however, is not the kind of power that the world applauds, for it is not vested in control, authority, and pride; rather, it is vested on the Word of God, and His promises of enabling. When

Jesus was led before Pilate during His crucifixion ordeal and trial, and He did not answer the governor's question as to who He really was, Pilate said to Him, *"Knowest thou not that I have the power to crucify thee, and the power to release thee?"* To this, Jesus replied, *"Thou couldst have no power at all against me, except it were given thee from [God]"* (John 19:10, 11, KJV). Pilate did not understand what was true power. He thought power was limited to political positions and authority. Sampson, the young Nazarene of biblical times, also felt that his power to destroy the powerful Philistines rested in something that was external—his long hair. That was until he sadly found out that his hair was simply a symbol of the real power of God in him to deliver His people from a heathen bondage.

The strength of God's children is the faith and trust that they place in the Great God of Heaven to do for, and through, them, those things that will bring glory to His name—the strength to resist sin; to overcome temptation; to trust in the face of fear; to walk in the darkness of despair; to hope, when there is no hint of help; to love, when the enemy is unlovely; and to forgive, when the offender is unforgiving. It is only as the Lord becomes our strength that we can receive power to do what seems unnatural. And that is true power!

Another dimension of this power is the joy that accompanies it—the Lord becomes the source of our joy and song. This type of power suggests victory over self and natural tendencies; hence, the joy that accompanies it is not generated from outside of us, but from within us. It is the joy that stems from abiding in the Lord. That power to be victorious and to be joyful is ours today, for it is a gift from God. Since power at any level generates a good feeling within the holder, claim that good feeling today, for nothing is impossible for you to do, and no one, and no situation, can take its power from you. This is a power that is personal, private, and beautiful.

Juliet, who is a brilliant, experienced Christian attorney today, recognized this very well many years ago. When she was studying at a European law school she declared to friends, and also to one of her professors who wanted her to compromise her ethical and religious values, that: "I cannot go contrary to my conscience if even it may cost me a coveted high grade." Although she ultimately earned her law degree, passed her law boards, and became a successful lawyer, her resolve at that time not to compromise her religious and ethical values did cost her the coveted high grade she wanted; but her strength and that power given to her by God resulted in a peculiarly high joy that she still remembers with deep delight and pleasure, even after almost thirty years.

Take hold of God's strength today and claim whatever power you need in your life as you bask in the promise of His accompanying song. Join the ancient prophet, Isaiah, today, and make the Lord your strength and your song. Take hold of that power!

POWER OF HOPE

*"And said unto him [Jesus], Art thou
he who should come, or do we look
for another?"*
(Matt 11:3, KJV)

Emily Dickinson, famous 20th century literary artist, known for her abstruse thought and reflections, crafted in poetry, a description of "hope." She portrays it as an abstract entity that lives in the heart. It gives a great feeling that propels people to undertake any challenge and gives joy even amidst pain and hurt. When that entity dies within the soul, however, there is little for which to live. Dickinson posits in the first verse of her poem, "Hope Is the Thing With Feathers":

> *Hope is the thing with feathers,*
> *That perches in the soul,*
> *And sings the tune without the words,*
> *And never stops at all.*

Hope brings joy no matter how dark the present looks. It is as necessary as breathing. There is a Latin proverb that says: *"Dum spiro spero"*, meaning, "while I breathe, I hope." Hope brings joy while life flows smoothly, but it also brings joy when life brings uncertainty. Jesus' disciples lived with this hope during the last days of their earthly time with Jesus. They were looking forward to an earthly kingdom in which they would have played a significant part. Jesus had to carefully remind them that His kingdom was not of this earth, for then they would have had to fight. (John 18:36). It took them a little time to understand this, but afterwards, they did.

Then there was John the Baptist, the forerunner and baptizer of Jesus. He was born for a specific task, which was to prepare the way for Jesus, our Savior and Lord. He preached in the wilderness as no one else ever did, and pointed everyone in his time to Jesus, the precious Lamb of God. He was subsequently arrested and taken into penal custody because of his preaching, teaching, and rebuking of sin in the lives of people everywhere. However, he was sure that Jesus, through His mighty and awesome power, would have done something miraculous to honor His divine name, and at the same time, deliver him from prison. So, he waited and waited, but nothing seemed to happen as the time approached for his execution.

Hope brings joy while life flows smoothly, but it also brings joy when life brings uncertainty.

All hope for his deliverance faded, and so he sent one of his disciples to look for Jesus and to ask Him if He were really and truly the Messiah, or whether there was going to be someone else. It so happened that on that very day, Jesus was busy teaching, preaching, and healing thousands, and casting out demons from many who were possessed. It was a long, hard, but glorious day for all (Matt. 8:1–34). When the messenger finally got to speak with Jesus, and delivered the query to Him from John, Jesus told him to return, and describe to John all that he had seen and heard that day. He did, and John was cheered and strengthened by divine power to keep his hope alive—a hope that transcended his earthly deliverance and embraced eternal joy and eternal life. The terror of death faded, and divine illumination dispelled the darkness of the executioner's axe, as Jesus declared to all who heard the messenger's query: *"Among those born of women there is no one greater than John"* (Luke 7:28, NIV).

Hope for the Christian never dies, even though sometimes the body may die. The power of hope transcends the darkness of earthly existence, and reaches into the luminous realms of eternal life, for when our eyes are open after our resurrection, the very first thing we will see is the wonderful face of our Lord and Savior, Jesus Christ! What a delight! What a joy! One anonymous poet puts it this way: "Hope sees the invisible, feels the intangible, and achieves the impossible." And it was Albert Einstein who declared: "Learn from yesterday, live for today, and hope for tomorrow."

God gives us the power to hope both in this life, and for life that will take place after the sleep of death. For now, however, trust Him to keep hope alive in your heart, today.

GOD, THE GREATEST EMPOWERER

> *"After this, I heard what sounded like the roar of a great multitude in heaven shouting: 'Hallelujah! Salvation and glory and power belong to our God."*
> **(Rev. 19:1, NIV)**

Only God could empower us to do what is seemingly difficult because He is the true source of all power—power belongs to Him! How wonderful it is to know that we are adopted sons and daughters of a God whose very name is Power! There is no limit to what He could do on earth, and no understanding of His immense power in Heaven. George Friedrich Handel identified vicariously with John the Revelator's statement, evidenced in Revelation 5:12 (KJV), when he declared in his immortal musical composition, *The Messiah*: "Blessing and honor and glory and power be unto Him who sitteth upon the throne ..."

Too often, we, as His earthly disciples, go about our lives in self-pity and worry as if we have no Heavenly Father who could take care of us when, all that is necessary, is a connecting line to Heaven that is easily strung through one cry for faith to trust God more. And if sometimes there is no faith because of the dense darkness of our night of pain, another cry would say to God: "Oh God, grant us that faith to believe in Your power!" When this happens, sunlight takes the place of darkness; despair turns to hope; jealousy becomes love; poverty is no more; sickness turns to health; and finally, we are given a glad today instead of a dreaded tomorrow.

There is no limit to the power of God in taking care of His children. This is why John the Revelator, even though faced with the loneliness and isolation of exile, and the possibility of imminent death, could have declared under the glow of a vision of the heavenly temple: *"Thou art worthy O Lord, to receive glory and honour and power"* (Rev. 4:11, KJV); and in a later narration of that stupendous scene, he commented: *"And the temple was filled with smoke from the glory of God, and from his power"* (Rev. 15:8, KJV).

Visiting with an upper-middle class, society prominent non-Christian gentleman several years ago, he expressed to me the thought that children of God do not know the true power that is available to them in this life. "If they only knew," he declared, "their lives would have been so much more happy, meaningful, and exciting, for this available power from an all-powerful God would keep one sitting on the edge of a seat, as it were, not knowing what to expect next in terms of exploits, achievements, successes, hope, and present peace in this turbulent world."

One cannot, therefore, help declaring: "Hallelujah!" whether life flows on like a river, or turns sour like a lemon. Power is there to rise above every situation; power is there to hope for a sunnier tomorrow; power is there to trust in the fiercest story; power is there to see a rainbow through the rain; power is there to trust a physically invisible God who reigns supreme in your heart and life, and who wants to give to all "*an expected end*" (Jer. 29:11, KJV).

> *One cannot, therefore, help declaring: "Hallelujah!" whether life flows on like a river, or turns sour like a lemon.*

The God of all power beckons you to trust Him today, and to vicariously share in experiencing what this power can do within you, and for you, as you live today, tomorrow, and forever with Him.

POWER TO ENDURE

"Behold, we count them happy which endure. Ye have heard of the patience of Job, and have seen the end of the Lord; that the Lord is very pitiful, and of tender mercy."
(James 5:11, KJV)

Endurance is not one of those virtues that comes easily and gives immediate joy. On the other hand, the word implies patience and longsuffering in situations that are un-ideal—situations with which the average, normal human mind cannot cope without regular encouragement and support from others. Even with these, sometimes, the mind goes awry, and those who are weak attempt, or commit suicide. They destroy themselves and bring sorrow to family members and others. From where can strength come? Clinical psychologists are trained to assist sufferers in this regard; school counselors and ecclesiastical clergy are also helpful to them, but ultimately, strength to endure must come from within the one who is going through the trial because of his or her personal relationship with God.

Endurance means, among other things, to remain firm and strong under suffering or misfortune without yielding; to undergo hardship without giving-in; to suffer; to bear continually, or to tolerate a negative situation. Such is never easy to do, naturally, but with God's strength, He can give the suffering one that power to endure until things change—as they often do. Nothing lasts forever no matter how endless that negative situation may appear to be. All things come to an end.

Some occasions that call for endurance include the following: caring for a sick mother or father with the Alzheimer's disease; caring for someone stricken with a stroke for several years; dealing with a wayward and disobedient son or daughter; being diagnosed with a serious fatal illness; waiting for a suitor in order to be happily married; awaiting the opportunity to bear a child; dealing with an unkind neighbor or so-called friend,' etc. The list is endless. However, whatever the trial, God can give the requested power to endure until He sees to free us otherwise; many times, we do not know what is behind the scene when God is in charge. We simply have to trust His providence and strength to see us through.

It was not and could not be easy for that ancient biblical character, Job, who lived in the ancient land of Uz, to have endured. He was no ordinary man; he was not only good, but a blameless and upright man who feared God and shunned evil: He was rich. He was the father of seven sons and three daughters, and owner of 7,000 sheep, 3,000 camels, 500 yoke of oxen, 500 donkeys, and a large number of servants. He was the greatest man who lived in that ancient land called Uz. His sons took turns holding great feasts in their homes at which time they invited their other brothers and sisters to eat and drink with them. When the period of feasts had run its course, it was then their dad's custom to sacrifice a burnt offering in their behalf. This all changed one day, however, when Satan and God had a personal confrontation over him, and God asked Satan if he ever considered His servant, Job. He was the epitome of all that was right and good. He was blameless and upright and hated evil.

Satan answered God by saying that Job was like that because he was receiving favors from Him, hence his righteous behavior, but that if He would only withhold any of these, Job would curse Him to His face (Job 1:11). Subsequently, the Great God of Heaven took on Satan's challenge. Someone living in today's world can hardly begin to even imagine how difficult it was for Job to endure the terrible disasters that Satan threw upon him, but God did not leave his servant alone; He gave him strength to endure. He will give it to you, too, when you ask Him.

First, news came to him through a messenger informing him, that during the course of that day, as his oxen were plowing and donkeys were grazing, the enemy Sabeans attacked and carried them all away; furthermore, they killed all the servants who watched over them, and that he—the messenger—was the only one who was able to run away. This news was obviously very devastating to Job, to say the least.

While he was yet giving this bad news, another messenger came to Job and said that fire from God fell from the sky and burned up all of his sheep and that he was the only shepherd who managed to escape to bring this news to him. Believe it or not, while this second messenger was still trying to describe to Job the details of this awful event, another messenger came and said to Job: *"The Chaldeans formed three raiding parties and swept down on your camels and made off with them. They put the servants to the sword, and I am the only one who has escaped to tell you"* (Job 1:17, NIV).

Incredibly, while he was still speaking, yet another messenger came and said to him: *"Your sons and daughters were feasting and drinking wine at the oldest brother's house when suddenly a mighty wind swept in from the desert and struck the four corners of the house. It collapsed on them and they are dead. I am escaped alone to tell you"* (Job 1:18–19, NIV). Not long after, Job realized that sores and oozing boils were breaking out all over his entire body to the extent that it was easier to remain naked throughout the day because of the itch and ooze. His situation was so bad, that his own wife, who should have been a means of strong emotional support, looked at her suffering "perfect" husband and declared: *"Dost thou still retain thy integrity? Curse God and die"* (Job 2:9, KJV). Job reprimanded her; then he got up from where he was sitting, tore off his clothes, shaved his head, fell to the ground, and cried out to God saying: *"Naked I came from my mother's womb, and naked I will depart. The Lord gave, and the Lord has taken away. may the name of the Lord be praised"* (Job 1:21, NIV). In all of these unbelievable trials, Job did not sin by charging God with wrong doing. No one else, apart from God, our great Creator, could have sustained Job in this series of experiences. He and He alone could have given him that power to endure.

Our lives on this earth will be tested in various degrees as we journey on. No two persons' trials may be the same, and our measure of strength to be faithful to the end will depend on our relationship with God. While it is totally unlikely that anyone will experience a trial like Job's living in the world of today, it is equally true that the magnitude and spiritual strength required in whatever may be our lot in this life will elicit total dependence on the power of God to endure. Evidences of such dependence are known to us through stories of travelers who journey on life's highways. Olive is a lovely, faithful, and committed Christian university professor, who revels in the ability to teach language and literature in a style that her students forever remember. She is one who knows God personally and loves and sacrifices for others constantly, but does not find it easy to love and care for her aged Christian mother, who, for almost thirty years has been stricken with the diseases of dementia and Alzheimer's. When one is just physically ill, he or she can show and demonstrate love, thankfulness, and appreciation to those who offer care, and this is satisfying to caregivers and other relatives and friends who visit; but when one cannot even recognize and appreciate love, care, and kindness shown them, and this condition goes on for scores of years, it is not at all easy on their children and others. Olive's mother is presently one century years old., but this now retired, Christian teacher is still faithful in patience and love. Such is an endurance that only God could supply.

> *Our lives on this earth will be tested in various degrees as we journey on. No two persons' trials may be the same, and our measure of strength to be faithful to the end will depend on our relationship with God.*

Kevin and Katherine did everything they knew in training their two lovely, young twin children to be obedient, polite, and kind. With one twin they struggled. They counseled, disciplined, prayed, and even cried out to God in his behalf, for they knew that if he did not change his behavior, he would end up getting in a lot of trouble with the law and even have to face imprisonment and shame. It took many years for them to see in him the positive traits they were working so hard to forge in him. Faithful friends encouraged them not to give up, but to keep on praying. Finally, and surprisingly, one day, a situation arose in the family that caused them to detect a completely different person in him; it was a character they had long wanted to see, an attitude that was the complete opposite to the child and young adult they knew. From then onward, Kevin was a rich blessing, joy, and delight to all. God had re-made him into a new creature, as it were, and people began speaking of him as the "old Kevin," and the "new Kevin," which at times became very amusing.

Yes, the intensity of Job's experience will never be ours, but as we deal with those situations in our own experiences that cause us great pain and appears as if they would never change, we have to ask the Great God and Father to grant us the power to endure, for if we do, most assuredly, joy will be our reward. Sometimes, we do not in our life-time experience seeing the change, but God will certainly grant us that joy when we see these results in God's heavenly kingdom. One way or the other, blessings come when we can, with His strength and power, endure. While endurance comes with pain, who is to know whether God and Satan had a conversation over us, and our love for, and our faithfulness to, Him? May we never disappoint Him!

The biblical account informs us that at the end of Job's story, he was richer than he was before, for God had helped him to endure. The Lord *"blessed the latter end of Job, more than his beginning: for he had fourteen thousand sheep, and six thousand camels, and a thousand yoke of oxen, and a thousand she asses. He had also seven sons and three daughters …. And in all the land were no women found so fair as the daughters of Job …. After this, lived Job an hundred and forty years, and saw his sons, and his sons' sons, even four generations. So Job died, being old and full of days"* (Job 42:12–17, KJV). May we ask God to give us today, that power to endure, regardless of the outcome!

THE POWER TO OVERCOME OBSTACLES

"With your help, I can advance against a troop; with my God I can scale a wall."
(Ps. 18:29, NIV)

Several years ago, in my quest to share the good news of salvation with others, I came across a rather genteel professional and aristocratic gentlemen, who listened engagingly to what I was trying to communicate. Then, with measured sentences, he said to me: "Ma'am, I want you to know that I do admire your understanding and interpretation of the Bible, but I want you to know that you have a power that you have not yet tapped within you but which I think you should explore. I want you to know that you can do anything that you please, if you would will yourself to do so through the process of reflection, meditation, and concentration." Needless to say, our conversation, though cordial, did not bear immediate fruits, but ultimately, with the passage of time, I was able to convince him that I depend, not only on my inner strength and power to accomplish anything, but on God's power.

It is amazing what we can accomplish physically and spiritually when we "hook up" with the mighty arm of God. Then our accomplishments will not be ours, but God's. In this Psalm, David was beside himself in joy and praise to God for delivering him from the hands of his enemies, and from the hand of King Saul. He, therefore, begins by saying: *"I love you. Lord, my strength"* (Ps. 18:1, NIV). Then he uses his great imagination to describe God's deliverance. His language is highly poetic: *"The cords of death entangled me; the torrents of destruction overwhelmed me. ... In my distress I called to the Lord"* (Ps. 18:4–6, NIV).

He then moves on to show, very powerfully, how God came to his deliverance. The highly figurative language describes with heightened impact God's intervention:

> *Then the earth shook and trembled; the foundations also of the hills moved and were shaken, because he was wroth. There went up a smoke out of his nostrils, and fire out of his mouth devoured: coals were kindled by it.... At the brightness that was before him his thick clouds passed, hail stones and coals of fire. The LORD also thundered in the heavens, and the Highest gave his voice; hail stones and coals of fire. Yea, he sent out his arrows, and scattered them; and he shot out lightning,*

and discomfited them.... He delivered me from my strong enemy, and from them which hated me: for they were too strong for me. (Ps. 18:7–8; 12–14; 17, KJV)

Then there is the quiet conclusion: *"Therefore will I give thanks unto thee, O LORD, among the heathen, and sing praises unto thy name"* (Ps. 18:49, KJV).

After every storm, there is a calm. After God intervenes, saves, and rescues, praise and thanksgiving should be given to Him. Power is available when we turn our situation over to God and cry out to Him for help. He then stands by us and delivers us in no mean manner, for we are precious to Him in an individual and personal way. May David's experience be yours vicariously, today!

THE POWER OF PRAYER

"Be careful for nothing, but in everything by prayer and supplication with thanksgiving, let your requests be made known unto God. And the peace of God, which passeth all understanding, shall keep your hearts and minds through Christ Jesus."
(Phil. 4:6, 7, KJV)

It is a well-known fact in the Christian world today, that the greatest power that we have is the power of prayer. One notable writer has declared that "more things are wrought by prayer than this world dreamed of."[6] The biblical records account for astronomical occurrences that were wrought only through this mighty power of prayer. These include, for example, Jesus feeding over five thousand men, women, and children with only five small barley loaves and two fishes; the man who was born blind and never was before able to see anything; the healing of the two blind men who came to Him for help to be able to see; the healing of the man who could not hear; the lame man who could not walk; the woman with the bleeding problem for over twelve years; the parting of the Red Sea so that millions of Israelites could have crossed over, then the returning of the waters that drowned all the Egyptians who pursued them; the deliverance of Daniel who remained unharmed after he was cast into a terrible den with hungry lions; the saving of the three Hebrew young men who were thrown in a fiery furnace that was made seven times hotter than before, yet they received not even a scorch; the resurrection of a man—Lazarus, who had died and was buried for four days; the opening of the natural eyes of Jesus' three disciples so they could have witnessed the glorious transfiguration of Jesus before He died; the answering of Hannah's prayer for a child after

---

[6] Alfred Lord Tennyson, *Idylls of the King*, 1859.

she pleaded in the temple, which resulted in the birth of Samuel—one of God's greatest prophets. These are just to name a few. The Holy Scriptures proliferate with an abundance of evidence for the mighty power of prayer.

"But that was long ago in the biblical times," I hear you say; "but what about me, today? Can God give me that power to trust in Him enough to answer the prayers I offer to Him, today? Do I have that same level of power?" God answers: "Yes, you do, for I am the source of that power, and whatsoever you ask of me, believing, you shall receive for the honor and glory of my name." *"Ask, and it will be given to you…"* (Matt. 7:7, NIV); *"And I will do whatever you ask in my name, so that the Father may be glorified in the Son. You may ask me for anything in my name, and I will do it"* (John 14: 13–14, NIV). The only channel we have for asking is through prayer—the talking to God as to a friend. Tell Him all that you would like Him to do for you, and ask Him for the faith to trust Him to do it. According to a boldly written sign on a public billboard: "Prayer is the world's greatest wireless connection." In concurrence, Deborah Dolen, a prolific writer in many genres, posits: *"There is power in prayer. It is the cheapest intangible asset we have and do not use enough of."* God's power, however, is never limited to historical periods, times, and circumstances. Prayer power is available to all—young or old; rich or poor. The difference lies in the trust and the faith that we place in Him to do what He says He will do.

I have had several personal experiences in my life when God has shown me the effectiveness of this *"power"* that He has given to His children, but one stands out predominantly. Several years ago, when I served as interim president of a Christian university in the Caribbean, two senior women called me up one day around noon to ask if I could substitute for someone who was requested and had agreed to fellowship with them at a women's retreat, and to take charge of a twilight open-air communion service. That person had a last-minute emergency and could not fulfill that assignment, and they were asking if I could fill in. I had never conducted a service like that in my life. I have taken part in scores of such services at several churches and in settings, but never was I in charge of one. Because of the circumstances, however, I reluctantly accepted this emergency request of the ladies, especially since it was a women's retreat in a secluded, mountainous area of that region. *No one will be watching to see what I did right, or what I did wrong*, I consoled myself.

All went well, and I myself was feeling blest. The singing was glorious and the testimonies very inspiring as the sun was just about ready to set in the distant west. We came to the end of the service, were just about ready to sing the closing hymn, when a young man, one of the only two who were there to help in lifting and moving beds and tables from room to room, politely approached and said: "Sister Mac (the shortened form for my surname—McGarrell), could you, before singing the closing hymn, pray for a young lady who is here, but is unwell. She is scheduled for surgery shortly, and her relatives who invited her to this Retreat, would like for her to be prayed for. Could you do that? She is not a member of our church." I kindly said to the young man, "*No.*" I told him I don't know the lady; have never seen her; she had not made a personal request of me; I am not a pastor; I have not been able to talk with her personally; we, as a church, do not practice public deliverance healing; I will need to talk with her on a personal spiritual and faith level; and we must sing our closing hymn now and bring this service to a close. After listening to me, he politely walked away.

After the service was over and I was getting ready to leave, two women came to me begging me to visit their retreat dormitory-type room to see how they had fixed-up their temporary dwelling. I acquiesced. After congratulating them for their creativity and "eye for beauty and loveliness," another two women approached me and my partner and asked the same favor. I did, and shortly after doing so, still another two did the same thing. While in that room, the same young man appeared on the scene and said, "Sister Mac, here is where the young lady I told you about earlier lives. She is here with her relative who invited her to this retreat."

"Where is she?" I asked.

"I'll go and get her," he replied. Shortly after, she appeared along with her relative. I asked her if she believed in the power of prayer. She said, "Yes; could you kindly pray for me? My doctors have diagnosed a cancerous tumor in my uterus, and I am due for surgery shortly, but I am afraid and do not want to do it."

I then called together the small group and shared the text: James 5:13 which says: *"Is anyone among you in trouble? Let them pray. Is anyone happy? Let them sing songs of praise. Is anyone among you sick? Let them call the elders of the church to pray over them and anoint them with oil in the name of the Lord. And the prayer offered in faith will make the sick person well; the Lord will raise them up. If they have sinned, they will be forgiven."*

"Do you believe this?" I asked her, and she replied, "Yes." I then prayed for her. The young man who had made the request in her behalf had in his pocket a small bottle of olive oil which he gave to me, and I anointed her forehead as I asked God's favor and healing power. I left that retreat area that night for my campus home feeling fully satisfied that I was able to do something I did not want to do, but God allowed circumstances outside of my control to allow me to perform a service I never did in my life. The way things worked out, I was convinced that God wanted me to do that.

Approximately two years passed on, and I forgot all about that experience as I got caught up in all my top administrative duties. One Sabbath after the divine service was over, however, and I was just about to walk down a short stairway from the auditorium where we worshipped, two women approached me and reminded me that they were the ones who invited me to conduct that communion service at the women's retreat a couple of years ago, and they wanted to give me an update on the young lady for, and with whom, I prayed for healing. "Dr. McGarrell," they said, "several good things have happened to her since you prayed. Among them are the following: 1) she requested another X-ray to be taken of her uterus, and it was discovered that it was clear of any tumor or cancerous invasion without the intervention of any surgical procedure; 2) she conceived and bore a lovely baby as if to prove that all was well; 3) she got married and became more happy and independent; 4) she got baptized into God's true Remnant Church; 5) she is now employed as a desk receptionist at our denomination's medical institution in the city of Port-of-Spain." It was too much for me to take in at one standing (I was still standing on the church's steps) to say the least. I simply lifted my soul to God and thanked Him, one more time, for the mighty *power of prayer*.

Several weeks after receiving this report, I went to the hospital's clinic for my usual bi-monthly check. As I sat with other patients waiting for my turn to come when my name would be called to see the doctor, a young woman came to me and said: "You are Dr. McGarrell, aren't you? I don't think you know or remember me, but I am the young lady for whom you prayed about two years ago for healing from cancer. I want you to know that many things have happened since then."

"Oh yes," I declared, rising from my seat to greet her, "I heard about your miracles from two women who came to our university church not long ago."

"Well," she continued, "there is a sequel to this experience which I don't think those ladies know. After receiving God's healing touch, I prayed and thanked God for using you to help; I then asked Him to use me to be of help to someone bringing hope and gladness just like He used you to do for me. God heard and answered.

"I had an old classmate friend with whom we had a 'falling out' since we were in high school, and we hadn't spoken to each other in many years. Somehow, my mind went on her, and I decided to search her out and pay her a surprise visit if possible. After making some inquiries, I was able to locate her. By this time, she was not married, but had two lovely little daughters, and life's circumstances were not kind to them—they had no money to live. As I rang her doorbell, she was surprised to see me. 'Well, what brought you here so suddenly after these many years?' she asked. 'I myself don't know, but my mind ran on you, and after making some inquiries, I decided to visit with you and to ask your forgiveness if I was the one who was responsible for the break in our girlhood friendship. You see, I joined the Seventh-day Adventist Church, and you know how those people are—they encourage the act of forgiveness no matter who is in the wrong. That is why I came because I remember what a strong friendship we shared before our relationship broke. I want you to know that life has never been the same for me since then.'

"After talking a little more and sharing a drink and some snacks, I told her I wanted to say a little prayer in her behalf, which I hoped she did not mind. She gladly agreed, and we then held hands as I prayed for her. As I approached the door to leave, she called me back and very emotionally said: 'You know, my friend, you said you joined a new church and that is what propelled you to search me out and pay me this visit; however, I want you to know that it is more than that. God sent you to visit with me. I am a woman with many problems and cannot support myself nor take care of my two daughters financially. I owe rent for several months, and my other bills are piling up; so I decided that I will put an eternal end to everything. I purchased some gramazone (poison used for killing weeds on a farm) and prepared three glasses for me and my two daughters—two small glasses and one large one. Come with me and I'll show you.'

"She then took me to her bedroom, and there on the lamp-stand stood the three glasses, two small ones three-quarters filled, and one large glass more than half way filled with the deadly stuff. 'When you came and rang my doorbell, I was just about going to distribute the deadly dose to the girls and after they die, I was going to drink mine. Your ring on my door disturbed all of this, and here we are now. I would never think of attempting such a stupid thing again. So, you think you just came, but I know God sent you just in time to save three lives.'"

She continued by saying, to me, "God used you to pray for, and heal me without surgical intervention, and I asked God to use me just like He used you, so that I can save the life of someone, too. God answered my prayer, and immediately I realized, in a renewed and stupendous manner, that there is 'power' in prayer." All of this was told to me by this young lady as I was still standing in the clinic amidst other outpatients as we were all waiting for our names to be called for our various doctors. Filled with deep emotion at all that was being relayed to me, I asked her if I could visit her office, which was located right behind the waiting room. She agreed and then led the way as I followed. There, together, we held hands and prayed as I thanked God for using her, the young lady for whom I prayed, approximately two years before, and who was now used by God so powerfully, in answer to her prayer to also be used by Him, to help others. Through my prayer, one person was made whole; but through her prayer, three were saved from untimely death. Never fail to make use of that wonderful available gift from God—the power of prayer!

"Power" is a gift that God has given to all of His children to be used, not for their personal aggrandizement or boastful pride, or human honor, but only for the honor and the glory of His name and the advancement of His cause here on earth. It has no limit. Societal positions, leadership craftsmanship, educational thrusts and achievements, physical beauty, personal honor, worldly fame, or media popularity are not a part of this power; rather, this is a power that is vested only in God, the All-powerful One, the only One who is omnipotent—full of true power; omniscient—all knowing; omnipresent—ever present; and omnificent—all creative. However, it is a gift that is achieved only by the asking of those who are humble and trusting in nature, as they enjoy a living, vibrant, and active relationship with a Great God and Father. Ask Him each day for that power! It will be your greatest joy and your greatest honor!

TEACH Services, Inc.
P U B L I S H I N G
www.TEACHServices.com • (800) 367-1844

We invite you to view the complete
selection of titles we publish at:
www.TEACHServices.com

We encourage you to write us
with your thoughts about this,
or any other book we publish at:
info@TEACHServices.com

TEACH Services' titles may be purchased in
bulk quantities for educational, fund-raising,
business, or promotional use.
bulksales@TEACHServices.com

Finally, if you are interested in seeing
your own book in print, please contact us at:
publishing@TEACHServices.com

We are happy to review your manuscript at no charge.